Original title:
The Poetry of Pines

Copyright © 2025 Creative Arts Management OÜ
All rights reserved.

Author: Atticus Thornton
ISBN HARDBACK: 978-1-80567-238-8
ISBN PAPERBACK: 978-1-80567-537-2

Tenderness in a Rugged Landscape

In the wild, they stand so tall,
With needles sharp, they catch a fall.
Squirrels dance, doing their best,
While branches whisper, 'Take a rest!'

Beneath the shade, the critters play,
Chasing dreams in a silly way.
The bark may be tough, but joy's alive,
In this forest where the giggles thrive.

Sighs of Resilient Armor

With coats of green, they keep it cool,
While raccoons plot and squirrels drool.
Their strength is shown in every sway,
Laughing off the winds of gray.

Roots deep down, they tickle the ground,
As creatures scurry all around.
Furry friends join in the cheer,
Underneath the sturdy spear.

Reflections on a Pine-Lined Path

Walking down this crooked lane,
I stop to giggle at a frog's campaign.
He croaks a tune while trees just sway,
Little do they know, it's a dance party day!

Each pine a guardian, tall and grand,
With shades so cool, they form a band.
A chipmunk winks, ready to glide,
On this joyful, pine-tree ride.

Nature's Own Lullaby

In the night, the pines hum low,
Like a secret song only they know.
The stars twinkle in a playful jest,
While owls giggle, taking their rest.

Crickets chirp with a comedic flair,
As the moonlight wobbles through the air.
With every breeze, there's laughter near,
In this serene, pine-scented sphere.

In the Heart of the Woodlands

In the heart of the woodlands, a tree struck a pose,
With branches like arms, it waved to the crows.
A squirrel swung by, in a acorn-stuffed coat,
Proclaiming his royalty, 'I'm the king of this grove!'

Moss tickles the trunks, it's a ticklish affair,
While birds sing a tune, with an outrageous flair.
The sun peeks through leaves, with a wink in its shine,
'Let's dance among shadows!' they cheerfully twine.

Pinecones and Moonlight

Under moonlit skies, the pinecones conspire,
To roll down the hills, oh what wild desire!
They bounce, they jive, making such a loud thud,
'We're just little warriors, ready for mud!'

The owls sit in laughter, with stories to tell,
While the pines sway along, in a rhythmic carousel.
A fox joins the fun, with a curtsy so spry,
'Join us, dear creatures, it's time to fly high!'

Sentinel Dreams

Tall sentinels standing, guarding the night,
Whispering secrets, 'Oh what a sight!'
They dream of adventures, of faraway lands,
Together they giggle, with rustling hands.

The raccoons are plotting a mischief brigade,
In their little tree homes, where shadows invade.
'Let's roll down the hills, next to the stream,
And capture the laughter of moonbeams that beam!'

Beneath the Boughs

Beneath the great boughs, where laughter is rife,
A party of critters celebrates life.
They toast with acorns and dance on the ground,
In this woodland hall, so joyful and round!

A badger brings snacks, with a grin ear to ear,
Saying, 'Don't mind the fuzz, it's the flavor we cheer!'
Together they tumble, in a colorful heap,
Under starlit skies, where the pines softly weep.

Veils of Mist on Pine-Laden Hills

Pines in pajamas, they sway and dance,
Their branches mess up, a wild romance.
Clouds roll in like a sneaky thief,
Dressing trees up, oh what a relief!

Misty veils hide the furry critters,
Squirrel's frolic, while the owl bitters.
Trees giggle softly, under misty shrouds,
Whispering tales to the curious crowds.

Resilience in the Face of Storm

A hurricane howls, but pines stand tall,
They've got a secret, tough barks for all.
With roots like anchors, they laugh at the breeze,
"Bring on your tempests, we'll do as we please!"

Branches may bend, but they never break,
Their humor's the cure, not a single mistake.
Each droplet of rain, they catch and they joke,
"I'm just giving the squirrels a nice humid soak!"

The Meeting of Earth and Sky

Pines reach for the clouds, heads held high,
"Hey, up there! Come play in the sky!"
With a sideways wink, and a whispered blurt,
"Why don't you hang out? Let's share a concert!"

The earth rolls in, where the pines all meet,
Tickling their roots with a warm, soft greet.
"Hey, neighbors, can we grow a bit closer?"
Bright laughter rings, as they get a little grosser.

Dreams in the Pine Needle Carpet

In a carpet of needles, dreams all sprout,
Mice host a party, there's no doubt.
With acorn confetti, and twinkling lights,
They giggle and dance into the starry nights.

While owls keep watch, with wise, goofy stares,
"Is that a party? I want to share!"
But those tricky pines just rustle and play,
"Sorry old friend, it's a needle ballet!"

Portrait of the Tall Sentinels

In the forest, they stand tall,
Brushing clouds, they have a ball.
Swinging left, then swinging right,
Tickling robins, what a sight!

Their outfits, green with little spikes,
Wearing hats made of birds' bikes.
Giggling at the squirrels' race,
Claiming all the sunlit space.

With roots like socks, they dig in deep,
Among them, secrets they do keep.
They sway and dance, but never break,
Hiding giggles 'neath every flake.

Guardians of the Mountains

Wrapped in bark, like ancient kings,
Counting the laughter that nature brings.
They guard the peaks with watchful grace,
Waving softly, like a friendly face.

Belly-laughs burst when wild winds blow,
Whispering secrets to the snow below.
They share their tips with the passing breeze,
'Sway with us, it's a joy to tease.'

Cheering on the climbing goats,
As they strut around in little coats.
Chasing shadows till the sun dips low,
Making mountains giggle in a row.

Nature's Whispering Spires

Pointing up to the sky so blue,
They joke with the clouds, who are quite the crew.
Tickling the stars with their fine-tipped leaves,
At night, they sing sweet lullabies with ease.

They sway and sway, a comical sight,
Waving to the owls, all through the night.
Stuck with a pine cone in their shoe,
They chuckle at what clumsy trees do!

In the quiet, they can plot and plan,
To confound the critters, their biggest fans.
They toss jokes down to the ants below,
While making shadows that dance and glow.

Breath of the Timbered Giants

With every breeze, their laughter flows,
Rustling softly where the wild grass grows.
They tell tall tales, both silly and grand,
As the sun tickles their boughs on land.

They wear crowns made of pine cone chapeaus,
Wishing for disco balls and flashy shows.
Their roots are tangled like a messy hair,
Yet they stand proud, without a care!

When critters scamper beneath their shade,
They tease, 'You think you'll find us afraid?'
These giants giggle, while the world spins round,
Gigantic jokesters, rooted in the ground.

Whispers Among the Needles

In the woods where the tall trees sway,
Pines gossip in a funny way.
"Did you hear about the squirrel's dance?"
"He tripped over a branch—what a chance!"

They chuckle as twigs snap and creak,
Laughing at birds who can't seem to speak.
A woodpecker's tap is a rhythmic joke,
As branches sway in a leafy cloak.

Symphony of the Silent Trunks

Beneath the boughs, a band assembles,
Where pine cones drop and laughter trembles.
The trunks attempt a woeful song,
But it's off-key, and they can't play long.

A deer prances in, trying to rap,
While squirrels roll on, in a gear-capped flap.
The melody's strange, but oh so witty,
Even the owls grin, and that's a pity!

Echoes in the Evergreen

In the deep green stretch, the echoes play,
Where trees throw shadows in a silly way.
A raccoon slips, and giggles ensue,
"Was that a moonwalk?" the pines woohoo!

Branches sway with jokes untold,
As beetles act out dramas bold.
Whispers float, all snickers and laughs,
Nature's own quirky, comedic staff.

Shadows Beneath the Canopy

Under the shade, the shadows dance,
With squirrels plotting their next prance.
They peek at sunbeams with giddy cheer,
Wishing for daylight to disappear!

The pines rustle in jest, it appears,
As whispers drift to eager ears.
"Is it a breeze or a joke from Fred?"
The trees snicker low, then shake their head.

Winter's Embrace on Evergreen Souls

Snowflakes fall with a silly dance,
Pines wear caps, it's their goofy chance.
Icicles hang like a frozen grin,
As squirrels chirp at their cozy kin.

Branches bow to a frosty jig,
They shake off snow like a wiggly wig.
Nature's kids play hide and seek,
While winter whispers, "Don't be meek!"

Glazed in white, they strike a pose,
With every gust, their laughter grows.
Winter's fun in the evergreens,
Brings giggles forth, like silly scenes.

The Melodies of a Whispering Wind

Breezes hum through the needle tips,
Pines whistle tunes, with funny quips.
Branches twist in a comical flow,
Swaying side to side, like vaudeville show.

Leaves attempt to join the beat,
But most just giggle, feeling their feet.
The wind blows harder, leaves tap dance,
It's a festive waltz; can you take a chance?

Songs of nature, a jazzy mix,
Where every tree has its silly tricks.
In a forest of chuckles, laughter weaves,
As melodies swirl in the cool evening leaves.

Pines in a Sea of Stars

Under the moon, pines jive with glee,
Stars blink brightly, setting them free.
Pines wear their best, a spiky attire,
Dancing wild, igniting the fire!

The squirrels join in, twirling so spry,
Chasing star dust as they leap high.
Pine cones fall with a plop and a wink,
Creating a chorus of fun as they shrink.

In the cosmic blend, trees laugh and sway,
Each star a joke, lighting up play.
A party of needles, a gala of light,
Where the universe chuckles in the night.

Under the Cloak of Spires

Spire-like pines touch the sky,
Wearing hats of cloud, oh my!
They gather whispers, sweet and spry,
While noodle-legged critters pass by.

Each branch is a stage for woodland tales,
With pigeons reciting, as humor prevails.
"Knock, knock!" they call, their jokes on cue,
While pine needles giggle, "Who's there? Boo!"

In this leafy theater, all take a seat,
As nature's jesters perform with fleet.
Under spire's cloak, the laughter grows,
A comedy club where anything flows.

Pines and the Echo of Time

In a forest where whispers grow,
Pines chuckle as they sway to and fro.
They tell tales of their pointy hats,
And argue about who's better at chats.

The squirrels take notes, oh what a tale!
One tree claims it once set sail.
But all know it just sways in delight,
As the winds tease it day and night.

Crickets play tunes, a silly show,
While trees giggle, putting on a glow.
Time is a trickster that likes to dance,
With the pines joining in at every chance.

So raise a toast to these tall, green friends,
Who laugh at life as the evening bends.
Let's cherish their mirth, their gossip and rhyme,
For they hold the secrets of echoing time.

A Tapestry Woven with Needles

In the woods where the needles tread,
A tapestry woven, not easily read.
Each thread is a story, quirky and sweet,
Of squirrels weaving dreams at pinewood feet.

One pine boasts of its stylish attire,
Crafted by birds who never tire.
A chipmunk chimes in, with a bead of sass,
"That hat's just a nest—come on, let it pass!"

The wind plays the harp, rustling the leaves,
While trees share their jokes, like a band of thieves.
They poke fun at the clouds drifting near,
"Look at those fluff balls; they're late to appear!"

With laughter resounding, they gather around,
Creating a symphony, joyful and sound.
In a world so serious, they dance and spin,
These needle-clad jesters, thick-skinned and thin.

Sonnet of the Swaying Giants

Oh giant pines, with your arms outstretched,
You dance in the breeze, all worries quenched.
Your needles whisper secrets, none can confine,
As the earth spins in circles, oh how you shine!

Branches adorn you, a leafy parade,
While birds practice songs in the shade you made.
Each summer the ants throw their yearly bash,
With pinecone confetti and snacks in a stash.

They boogie and wiggle, oh what a sight,
While you stand there, giggling, with all your might.
Those birds take their bows, proud of their show,
Making you chuckle, for they steal the flow.

Yet still, here you stand, with roots dug in deep,
While dreams of the forest swirl up like heaps.
The giants sway gently, a comedy act,
In the spotlight of moonlight, no humor they lack.

The Pathway to Forgotten Realms

On a pathway lined with plush green pines,
Stories spill out like overcooked lines.
Each step a mischief, a laugh, a charm,
While woodland critters offer a calm.

The pines point ways to realms lost in cheer,
Where shadows dance lightly and thrive without fear.
"Hey, bring out the cookies!" one pine will shout,
While the breeze joins the party, twirling about.

With laughter erupting, the owls will agree,
"This path leads to wonders, come play and be free!"
The mushrooms all chuckle, wear spots with flair,
As the dancer delights, it forgets all its care.

So wander these woodlands, for fun is a must,
When the pines tell a story, it's bound to adjust.
In their forest of echoes, where all canberam,
Join in their laughter; it's pure, never bland.

Heartbeats of the Arboreal World

Among the trees, I dance and prance,
The branches sway, they join the chance.
Needles point like fingers fine,
Tickling thoughts with every line.

Squirrels plan their cheeky heist,
Gathering nuts, oh what a feast!
But slips and falls are part of fun,
Nature laughs—yes, we've begun!

A rustling sound, a gentle tease,
Pinecones drop like whispered pleas.
They land with thuds that echo loud,
Pine's playlist for the forest crowd!

So here's to pines, their quirky ways,
In every breeze, a joke or praise.
Let's sway and giggle, join this spree,
In this green jest, we're wild and free.

The Stillness of Pine Groves

In quiet groves where shadows play,
The pines seem to whisper all day.
With every wind, they rise and sway,
Mimicking secrets, come what may.

A woodpecker's tap in a solemn tone,
Makes all the pines feel less alone.
"I'm telling jokes, so come be near!"
But all they get is a blank stare here!

The squirrels gossip, they plan their tricks,
Plotting escapades like little flicks.
Meanwhile, pine needles fall like rain,
Soft jokes from trees—why so much pain?

Yet still they stand, proud, tall, and bright,
With bark as armor in the night.
Pine trees grin with wisdom bright,
And hum their tunes to make things right.

Love Letters in Fir and Spruce

In twinkling lights of woodland's heart,
Fir trees write, their love aart.
With every needle, a note they send,
A sweet reminder, trees can mend.

"Dear Spruce," one pine wrote with flair,
"Your branches beckon, I'm in despair!
Would you join me for a winter's night,
To snuggle close, it feels so right?"

"Dear Pine," replied, with a gentle sway,
"Your aroma is a bouquet today!
Let's dance together, just you and me,
Under the moon, and free as can be."

And so their love in needles grew,
Filled with laughter, and morning dew.
A couple bound by forest decree,
Love letters penned in majesty.

Nature's Green Poem

Nature's pen moves swift and free,
In pages green, she leaves for me.
Lines of laughter, sprigs of cheer,
In piney scents, her voice is clear.

With every breeze, she writes a verse,
Of squirrels' antics and forest curse.
"Why did the pine cross the way?
To shine on stage, it's its big day!"

Her poetry flows in knotted roots,
And every pine grows its own cute shoots.
While dancing shadows play their role,
Nature's jokes weave through each soul.

So if you stroll through this grand art,
Feel the whispers that touch your heart.
The trees will chuckle, the winds will jest,
In this green poem, we're truly blessed.

Memories Painted in Green Hues

In the forest, laughter echoes,
Squirrels play hide and seek,
Pine needles tickle our toes,
Nature's charm is truly unique.

The trees gossip as we pass,
Whispering secrets, oh so dear,
With each step upon the grass,
Joyful tales fill the atmosphere.

Branches dance in a gentle breeze,
While birds sing silly little songs,
With every rustle, hearts are at ease,
And time just drifts along.

A pinecone falls with a thud,
On unsuspecting heads, they land,
In this forest, life's a crud,
But oh, isn't it just grand?

The Voice of the Old Growth

Listen close to the wise old trees,
They murmur tales of yesteryear,
With leafy caps, they sway with ease,
Their laughter ticks like antique gears.

A woodpecker's pecking beats a tune,
Echoing through the vibrant wood,
Pine needles sway beneath the moon,
Chirping critters add to the mood.

Old branches stretch, creak, and crack,
As if cracking jokes from times gone by,
Yet in their shade, we never lack,
For joy has roots that never die.

A comedy show that nature brings,
With every gust, the pines do sway,
In their presence, laughter sings,
Beneath these giants, we laugh and play.

Fragrance of Faithful Roots

Oh, the scent of pine fills the air,
Like a cologne from decades past,
Each whiff brings memories to share,
Nostalgic moments, forever cast.

Ants march in a comical line,
Under branches, they strut with pride,
In this kingdom, they're just fine,
Among the roots, their fun they hide.

Sunbeams poke through the piney crown,
Creating a patchwork on the ground,
Dancing shadows, they twirl around,
In this forest, joy is found.

Take a breath, let the pine scent in,
It's like laughter bottled in a can,
There's magic in where the trees begin,
And adventure awaits, yes, it can!

The Stand of Timeless Watchers

Standing tall, with a grin so wide,
The pines have seen a funny thing,
With acorns firing like a slide,
In their shade, every heart takes wing.

Chirps and squeaks turn into grand shows,
As the critters prance in a race,
With nimble feet, they steal the prose,
While the trees just laugh in their place.

Branches stretch like arms in cheer,
Inviting all to join the fun,
A gathering of friends so dear,
In this stand, there's room for everyone.

So here's to the trees, wise and old,
Their laughter hanging in the air,
With every tale that they have told,
Our own stories intertwine with care.

Echoes Through the Silent Woods

In the forest where whispers grow,
Pines gossip softly, quite the show.
They crack jokes with the breeze in flight,
Bending low, they chuckle in delight.

Squirrels sneak by, with acorn treats,
While trees roll their eyes at noisy feats.
Each needle laughs in the soft sunlight,
As shadows dance and the day turns bright.

Branches sway, they can't keep still,
Tickling the clouds with a quiet thrill.
Whispers echo with a hearty cheer,
It's the best comedy show of the year!

So if you wander through this green stage,
Listen closely to nature's page.
Laughter rustles through leaves on high,
A merry tune beneath the sky.

When the Needles Kiss the Sky

Needles point up, a quirky trend,
Stretching so tall, they don't pretend.
"Look at us!" they seem to say,
"We're the tallest in the green ballet!"

The sun peeks in, then ducking out,
While branches stretch and twist about.
Each pine wears crowns of pointy glee,
In this tall game of peek-a-boo spree.

Raindrops tumble, a splatter of fun,
While needles dance in the afternoon sun.
"Did you see that? I caught a drip!"
They giggle as water takes a slip.

So next time you're hiking, take a peek,
At these silly trees that love to speak.
Kiss the sky, they cheerfully shout,
"Join us in our leafy night out!"

Guardians of the Mountain Air

Pines stand tall, like sentinels grand,
Guarding the secrets of the land.
With roots like a spider's web so wide,
They chuckle together, their knobby pride.

Clouds come floating, a fluffy parade,
While pines gossip in the cool shade.
"Did you hear that? A bird just said,
It's a weird life, but we're well-fed!"

Mountain air tickles each needle's tip,
As the trees share tales with an amusing quip.
"Remember that time we saw a goat?
He thought he could dance; he missed the boat!"

So here in the heights, the laughter spry,
With each breeze passing, the pines comply.
Guardians of humor, through night and day,
In these mountain woods, they always play.

A Dance of Green Against the Blue

When the sun spills gold, oh what a sight,
Pines sway in rhythm, a joyful flight.
Dancing to breezes, they take a bow,
"Can you keep up?" they quip with a wow!

Each twist and turn, a leafy parade,
While shadows play games in nature's arcade.
"Look at us spin!" the tall ones boast,
As the clouds pass by, they toast and coast.

Grass giggles low, joining the fun,
While flowers cheer, "Aren't they the one?"
Together they whirl in a laughter spree,
A tapestry winks, from land to sea.

So when you see them dance, take a chance,
Join the fun, give the trees a glance.
For in this green scape, joy takes flight,
A merry waltz under skies so bright.

Tales of the Tall Pines

Once stood a pine, so very tall,
It danced in the wind, and forgot its fall.
With branches that waved and did not care,
It teased the clouds, 'Come down if you dare!'

Squirrels held meetings up high in the leaves,
Plotting their snacks and all autumn thieves.
The pine just chuckled, said, 'Join in my fun,
We'll throw acorns at folks who walk in the sun!'

Oh, what a tale of a tree so spry,
That tickled the birds, as they flew by.
With trunks wearing laughter, and roots full of glee,
It reminded us all, stay light like a bee!

So if you find one standing so proud,
Wave at the pine, join the rowdy crowd.
With a wink and a nod, it'll whisper to you,
Life's better with laughter, that much is true!

Raindrops and Resin

Pitter-patter rain on the pine's leafy hat,
It giggled and danced, oh, how it sat!
With droplets that tickled its thick, green skin,
Each splash was a joke, let the fun begin!

Resinous laughter filled the damp, still air,
As the pine told the raindrops, 'You must beware!'
For once I was sticky, a sap-slinging show,
Got stuck to a squirrel, oh, he didn't know!

A deer trotted past, slipping on my glee,
I laughed so hard, left a knot in my tee!
The raindrops just tumbled, in fits of delight,
As the pine stood there, its trunk held tight.

So next time it rains, look up at the trees,
Join in the antics, and dance with the breeze.
For nature's a stage, where good humor thrives,
Even the tallest, they jump and they jive!

Whispers of an Evergreen

In the woods where the forest is calm and green,
An evergreen chuckled, a sight to be seen.
'Come gather around, I've stories to tell,
Of squirrels and fog, and where acorns fell!'

With needles like quills, it penned down its fate,
The wind whispered secrets; it couldn't wait.
'Oh, I once had a hat, made of snow and of sun,
It melted away, but we had had such fun!'

The critters below rollicked and swayed,
Under a tree that forever stayed.
With a wink and a nod, the whispers grew loud,
Like a pine-scented hug wrapping the woodsy crowd!

So when you're out wandering, take a deep breath,
Listen to stories of laughter, not death.
For every tall tree has a song to impart,
We're all just a laughter-filled moment apart!

Symphony of Needle and Bark

With a rustle and crackle, the pines sway and play,
A symphony crafted in the bright light of day.
Their needles are the strings, and the bark, oh so fine,
Creating a concert of humor divine!

The wind it hums softly, the sap starts to dance,
Each bend in the branches gives laughter a chance.
Frisky little squirrels take turns on the stage,
And trees all around them shout, 'Act your age!'

When water drops glisten, it's the percussion they need,
As the pine tries to whistle, but ends up with speed.
A ruckus of giggles, what a comical sound,
With every sweet note, joy and laughter abound!

So let's raise a glass to the tall, lovely trees,
Their symphonies linger with a light, breezy tease.
In every green corner where nature will spark,
Lives a funny old tale, sung by needle and bark!

The Spirit of Solitude in the Woods

In the woods where trees feel grand,
A squirrel dreams of a rock band.
Branching out, they strum and play,
Playing tunes in a leafy sway.

The sun peeks through in beams of gold,
While chatting trees share tales retold.
One's a poet, on bark they write,
Dreaming of fame in the moonlit night.

A tidy path they claim with pride,
But all get lost, none can decide.
Their shadows dance in silly glee,
Making fun of lost symmetry.

So if you wander with a grin,
Embrace the noise, let laughter win.
The solo act is not quite true,
For nature's joke includes you too.

A Journey Through an Arboreal Maze

I wandered deep where trees conspire,
Each twist and turn ignites my fire.
A map, I thought, would be my tool,
But trees just laughed, 'You silly fool.'

Branches wave like hands in cheer,
'Come this way, or maybe here?'
A raccoon pops up, gives a wink,
'Get lost? Well, that's the trees' main kink!'

Creeping vines tried to ensnare,
But I danced right through without a care.
'What's this place?' I shouted loud,
The pines replied, 'We're quite proud.'

In this maze of green delight,
Every turn's a party night.
So if you stumble, don't you fret,
Just join the trees—let's laugh, not sweat!

Flourish of the Evergreen Heart

Amongst the pines, a party waits,
Just watch them sway with wiggly traits.
Dancing roots and wiggly bark,
Their evergreen antics light the park.

A pinecone pranks with a cheeky roll,
Saying, 'I'm more than just a whole!'
While needles fall like confetti rain,
Creating a carpet, a crazy chain.

Pine perfumes are wafting by,
As squirrels plug their ears and sigh.
They think, 'These trees have lost their glee,'
But nature laughs—it's all carefree.

So join the fun, don't stand apart,
Feel the rhythm of nature's heart.
In every breeze, a giggle found,
When evergreen spirits gather 'round.'

Lyrical Shadows Beneath Tall Pines

Under tall pines, shadows mix,
They tell their tales with clever tricks.
One says, 'I'm a poet bold!'
The other sighs, 'That story's old.'

The rin of laughter floats along,
As branches sway like a dance song.
Feathers of leaves play peek-a-boo,
While squirrels strut, showing off their 'hue.'

A mystery game they love to play,
Hide and seek for night and day.
Bark covered sprites with grins so wide,
Invite you in to jolly hide.

So come join in this game of fun,
Beneath the pines, let's laugh and run.
With every heartful, giddy cheer,
Embrace the shadows, let's appear!

Between Silence and the Breeze

The pines stand tall, like guards on duty,
Whispering secrets, oh so fruity.
Their needles dance in a laughing cheer,
As squirrels debate who's got the better idea.

A pinecone drops—a thud, not a thump,
The ground shakes slightly, there's no need to jump.
Nature's own humor, it rolls with glee,
As the wind joins in, oh can't you see?

Pine sap glistens like glue gone wild,
Sticky and sweet, like a misbehaved child.
The breeze teases branches, a playful embrace,
While birds hop around in a musical race.

They hold their meetings, in whispers divine,
Sharing tall tales of sun and of wine.
The laughter of pines makes the cold air warm,
In a world so serious, they bring the charm.

Chronicles of Resin and Rain

Once upon a time in a forest so bright,
Pines told their stories, oh what a sight!
Resin like treasure, it dripped with delight,
Making mushrooms giggle, yeah, what a night!

The rain came to play, with a splash and a plop,
The pines took cover, but never would stop.
Dancing in raindrops, they twirled all around,
Making puddles shimmer; a splashing sound.

Digging up old roots, they'd tell with a grin,
Of how they'd once hosted a whole woodland inn.
Where critters all gathered, their stories a feast,
A community born in a trunk of the least.

So, if you wander where the pines stay green,
Listen for laughter, it's quite the scene.
The rain and the resin, a messy romance,
In this woodsy theater, join in, take a chance!

Dialogues with the Ancient Holders

Oh ancient trees, with wisdom to spare,
What secrets of life are tangled in hair?
The pines chuckle softly, a rustling sound,
"Just enjoy the breeze, let joy abound!"

They gossip and bake under sun's warm embrace,
Sharing tall tales at a casual pace.
"Did you see that bird? Look at him show!
He thinks he's a piper, with no place to go!"

"Remember the storm?" one pine starts to sigh,
"The way we danced, oh, we reached for the sky!
And when the thunder rolled, did you see me sway?
I could've sworn I pulled a branch the wrong way!"

So gather 'round pines, with laughter so clear,
For wisdom is funny when friends gather near.
They may seem so serious, rooted in grace,
But oh how they chuckle when you join the race!

A Canopy of Timeless Reflections

Underneath the pines, where the shadows play,
Reflections of laughter chase worries away.
Their trunks are like mirrors, with stories to share,
Pointing at clouds—"Look! The bunny's up there!"

A squirrel complains, "My acorn's gone poof!"
The pines quiver softly, then burst into woof!
"Did you check near the roots? That's where they all fall,
You've got to be quick, or you'll miss the small!"

They watch as the kids play beneath leafy halls,
A canopy woven with giggles and calls.
"Each step's an adventure, now look at them go,
They think we're just trees, but oh how we know!"

So if you need humor, just sit for a while,
The pines will enchant you, and coax out a smile.
In their timeless embrace, life dances and sings,
Underneath the pines, oh the joy that it brings!

A Chorus of Soft Needles

In the forest, trees stand tall,
Whispering secrets, oh what a ball!
Their needles dance, twirling with glee,
Singing tunes, just like you and me.

Squirrels chat, in joyful delight,
Stealing acorns, oh what a sight!
Pines giggle, as branches sway,
"Catch me if you can!" they seem to say.

Underneath, a carpet of green,
What a funny, leafy scene!
They poke at passing birds with ease,
"Come join us, dance among the leaves!"

Oh, the laughter in the cool pine air,
Making jokes without a care.
A chorus of needles, soft and bright,
In the forest, everything feels just right.

Swaying in the Breeze

Pines are twirling, shaking away,
Swaying gently, come join the play!
Their branches wave like they've got style,
Bowing down, they wink with a smile.

A ladybug slips down a green track,
Heading for fun, never looking back.
"Let's roll, let's rock, let's rejoice!"
The pines chime in with a newfound voice.

In the breeze, they take a twirl,
Mossy soft carpets start to swirl.
"Hey, who's the best dressed?" they jest,
With bark suits, they specify their quest.

With laughter echoing all around,
Nature's humor in each sound.
Swaying gently, keeping the beat,
In a woodland disco, life is sweet!

Radiance of the Resilient

Tall and proud, they reach for the light,
Strutting their stuff, what a sight!
With needles shining, oh so glow,
They make the sun go 'Wow!' and 'Whoa!'

A pine cone drops, plops on my hat,
"Good aim!" I shout, "Just like that!"
With a chuckle, the pines reply,
"We're the best, don't you deny!"

Wind tickles each needle, they giggle and sway,
"Join the party, don't you stray!"
Radiance beams from every tree,
"Hooray for us, can't you see?"

Amidst the laughter, life breezes by,
With nature's punchlines, oh my, oh my!
Each resilient tree, bold and free,
Brightens the day, just you and me.

Song of the Pine Forest

In the heart of the woods, they sing away,
A quirky chorus, come what may!
Pines hold auditions, calling each feline,
"You'll find our talent truly divine!"

With every rustle, a comedic play,
"Did you hear that? What did they say?"
The trees break into fits of their own,
"We're not just trees; we're pines with tone!"

A bird joins in, a whistling show,
And soon the pines put on a full-blown glow.
"Who knew trees could carry a tune?"
As critters gather, morning to noon.

So here's to the giggles in every bark,
The woodland symphony, make your mark!
In a tree-top theater, filled with cheer,
The song of the forest brings us near!

Embrace of the Tall Sentinels

In a forest so lush, trees dance and sway,
They tickle their neighbors in the silliest way.
Pine cones drop down like nature's own bombs,
While squirrels hold court in their leafy colms.

Their needles are sharp, but their humor is bright,
They joke of the clouds that float past in flight.
With trunks like great giants, they wiggle and bend,
In a game of hide-and-seek, they never quite end.

Branches reach out for a slapstick embrace,
As birds chirp along in their feathery race.
Each gust of the wind starts a giggle or two,
While critters below play peek-a-boo too.

In this green comedy, all stand in a row,
With laughter like echoes that twinkle and flow.
Nature's tall jesters, so proud and so free,
Join in on the fun—come and swing by a tree!

Shadows Beneath the Canopy

Beneath the tall trees, shadows stretch wide,
Where creatures concoct their odd genus of pride.
A raccoon in shades holds a tea party grand,
While ants in a line play the odd marching band.

The sunbeams peek down, they knit laughter and glow,
As chirps and croaks join the improviso show.
A turtle just winks, with a slow-motion grin,
Saying, 'Life's in the fun, let the games begin!'

A squirrel dons glasses, reads tales from the wood,
With plot twists and punchlines that are rather good.
The ferns sway in rhythm, the moss hums a tune,
While shadows dance freely, making shapes like a cartoon.

In this theatrical space, life's roles are reversed,
Each shadow is giggling, but are they well-versed?
With nature's own script, all antics unwind,
The laughter resounds, leaving worries behind!

Swaying Elegance in the Breeze

Pines stand with flair, in their green tuxedos,
Ready for parties, with an audience of meadows.
Their branches are arms that sway wildly with grace,
While the breeze tells a joke with a ticklish embrace.

A gust gives a twist, and the needles all wiggle,
Creating a rhythm that makes all hearts giggle.
Each rustle's a laugh, a whisper so gleeful,
As trees share their tales, like a council of people.

With roots planted firm, yet their tops feel the dance,
They sway with the giggles, they toss and they prance.
Cone hats worn proudly, they spin with delight,
As critters below find their moves pure and right.

Here's to this waltz in the wind's cheery tune,
Pines quote their own wisdom beneath the bright moon.
In this fun-loving grove, let your worries unfreeze,
Join the swaying elegance brought in by the breeze!

Secrets Held by the Forest's Spine

In the depths of the woods, secrets are sly,
Where trees whisper tales as they reach for the sky.
A woodpecker knocks, like a drummer on call,
Sharing gossip of critters that scurry and crawl.

From whispers of roots to acorns that plot,
The forest's a stage where intrigue is hot.
Spiders weave stories in silken delight,
While owls in the night blink wise, with insight.

In shadows they gather, the wise and the frail,
Sharing quips of the breeze in their leafy traile.
And the pines, with their stature, digest all the fun,
As laughter cascades, like rays from the sun.

So jog through the trees where secrets unfold,
In whispers and giggles, let joy be retold.
For nature concocts its own riddle divine,
In this whispering world, let your heart intertwine!

The Magic Woven in Green

In a forest where trees wear hats,
The squirrels tell jokes to playful cats.
Leaves dance around with a rustling cheer,
All the critters giggle, so sincere.

A trunk that can sway like a bouncy child,
Roots go for walks, oh so wild.
Acorns play hopscotch on mossy stones,
While the pinecones chuckle in silly tones.

Branches play tag with the breeze at night,
Whispering secrets of joy and delight.
Sunbeams peek through, painting bright scenes,
Nature's grand theatre, where laughter convenes.

In this kingdom of needles and green,
Laughter's the crown, forever unseen.
So next time you stroll, don't miss the show,
Join in the fun, let your laughter flow!

Enchantment in the Softest Whisper

Tickling the sky, the tall ones stand,
With needles so soft, they make quite a band.
Whispers of yarn spun from forest dreams,
In the quiet of twilight, nothing's as it seems.

Beneath their green umbrellas, we gather round,
Cricky crickets join in, a symphony sound.
When pine trees hold hands, what wonders they share,
Giggles and chuckles float up in the air.

The wind laughs too, adding some zest,
In this party of pines, all are a guest.
Creating such mirth in the cool evening haze,
Nature's own jester, in so many ways.

So if you hear laughter from trees up so high,
Just know it's the pines, with a wink to the sky.
Jump in their party, find humor in strife,
In the heart of the woods, there's magic in life!

Sentinels of the Ancient Way

Guardians of giggles in green-gowned grace,
They stand tall and proud, forming a place.
With roots like dancers, they sway to the tune,
The sun's bright laughter bursts out like a balloon.

Old as the stories of wisdom and lore,
They chuckle at time, wanting nothing more.
A breeze flips their leaves, they shimmy and shake,
Oh watch out, dear friend, or you might just break!

They hoard all the secrets of tricksters and jest,
While critters approach for a wise comedy fest.
Branches extend in an invitation sweet,
Hop on the fun train, take a seat!

In their shade, every giggle's a treat,
As nature spins jokes, oh what a feat!
With sentinels standing, laughter will stay,
In the embrace of these legends, come play!

Ink and Needles

In the sketch of the forest where ink flows bright,
Pines scribble their tales under the moonlight.
With needles that stitch every whim and delight,
Crafting a tapestry of laughter, just right.

Doodles of critters, they spring into view,
A wily old fox sporting one shoe.
While owls wear glasses, reading the scene,
In the book of the woods, where giggles convene.

Ink spills like giggles, over pages of green,
Whispers of pines craft a playful scene.
In this amusing quill, nature quakes,
With scribbles and chuckles, it's fun that it makes.

So come grab a brush, and join in the spree,
Paint with the laughter, wild and free!
Ink and needles, in a world quite divine,
Celebrate humor in every pine line!

Flickers of Sunlight Through the Foliage

When little critters dance around,
They twirl beneath the trees unbound.
The sun sneaks in with laughter bright,
Making shadows giggle with delight.

Beneath the needles, jokes are spun,
Squirrels debate who's the fastest run.
A woodpecker joins, tapping a beat,
To see who will admit defeat.

The breeze joins in with a silly cheer,
Whispering secrets only they hear.
And though the branches sway and play,
They won't give up on a funny day!

The pines all chuckle at the sight,
As nature puts on a comical show so bright.

Requiem for the Ancient Wood

In a forest where clocks seem to freeze,
Old trees wear hats made of leaves.
They tell tales of days long gone,
Of squirrels who thought they could fawn.

"Hey! You think you can outlast me?"
A mighty oak booms with glee.
The pines chime in with a chuckle low,
"We've seen seasons come, just watch us go!"

A twist and shout of branches sway,
The lizards join, trying to play.
Each tree bustles with history vast,
Yet here they stand, tilting heads at last.

With humor hidden in bark's embrace,
They pass the time at a leisurely pace.

Nestled in the Heart of Silence

In silence steeped, a snicker grows,
Where pines stand tall, in tidy rows.
A rabbit peeks, adjusting its ear,
Wondering what gossip's drawing near.

Whispers float on the evening air,
As critters gather without a care.
"Did you hear the tales of the man in red?"
"He wore pine needles upon his head!"

They chuckle softly, a flicker of laughs,
Debating the best nature crafts.
A chipmunk boasts of its acorn stash,
While the trees sway, a rhythmic bash.

All the secrets of the serene trees,
Are wrapped in laughter and gentle breeze.

The Heartbeat of the Untamed Wild

With every pulse, the forest shakes,
As twigs snap under playful jakes.
The wildest party, this land professes,
Where furry dancers wear leafy dresses.

"Let's spin around till dawn's first light,"
Cries a pinecone, feeling quite bright.
Fawns leap in with a springy grace,
Taking the lead in this silly race.

Old branches hang like laughs in the air,
Echoing tales with a fanciful flair.
And in this realm, where laughter thrives,
Each heartbeat plays, and nature jives.

A Tapestry of Green

Tall and pointy, waving around,
They're masters of fun, in leafy crown.
Whispering jokes in the summer air,
Tickling the squirrels with gentle flair.

Little birds laugh as they swing high,
In the breeze they give a sly wink and sigh.
A trunk's great grin, in bark so rough,
Stealing the scene, isn't that enough?

Oh, the shadows they cast on the ground,
It's a cool party that rarely's found.
Each needle a tickle to those who pass,
Forest shenanigans, nothing but sass!

Their comedy thrives when the wind gets bold,
A rustling giggle, a story retold.
Nature's comedians, they never quit,
Those pines stand tall, always a hit!

The Language of Conifers

Did you hear the pine trees speak with glee?
They share the gossip of every bee.
In whispers and giggles, secrets they keep,
As the chipmunks gather, they start to leap.

Cones are their letters, scattered around,
Quirky messages in the soft ground.
Branches play tag with the wayward breeze,
What a funny sight, if you please!

When the snowflakes fall, they wear a white hat,
Like a birthday party, imagine that!
They stomp and dance when the storms roll through,
Nature's comedies, fresh and new.

In the quiet dusk, they tell their tales,
Of happy squirrels and mischievous snails.
Their laughter echoes, a joyful din,
In the world of greens, they sure know how to win!

Secrets of the Wind-Swept Pines

With a swagger and sway, the pines command,
Secrets of the forest, they help to expand.
Tales of the critters, of laughter and fun,
Every gust of wind says, 'Come join the run!'

Bouncing and flouncing, their needles confide,
As the sun plays peekaboo from inside.
Cracking a joke when the branches collide,
A woodland comedy, no place to hide!

Through the rustling leaves, the whispers abound,
Pine antics echoing all around.
Who knew they could gossip with such a flair?
While standing so tall, they spread joy in the air!

So sway with the pines, catch a giggle or two,
Their secrets are magic in the evening dew.
Dance with the shadows, let laughter ignite,
The pines are the jesters, in a tree-filled delight!

Dancing Aromas of the Forest

Pine-scented humor in the breeze it flows,
Aromatic tickles from the trees it grows.
They twirl and giggle, the needles so bright,
Turning the forest into a laugh-filled sight.

Swaying in rhythm, what a lovely dance,
They prance and they preen in a leafy romance.
The sap drips a story, so sticky and sweet,
While the rabbits hop by with joy in their feet.

In the sun-soaked clearing, they twinkle and shine,
Those conifers know how to throw a good time!
With pinecone confetti all scattered around,
Celebrating life in a joyous sound!

From dawn until dusk, they revive the lore,
Of woodland giggles and legends of yore.
So join in the fun, let it echo and ring,
For the dancing aromas have much joy to bring!

Lament of the Timeless Trees

Oh, the trees stand tall, with wisdom so grand,
Yet they've seen more seasons than we can comprehend.
With roots in the earth, they wiggle their toes,
Complaining about squirrels who dance on their nose!

Once a branch got a splinter, it cried with dismay,
"I'm stuck in this posture, will I ever sway?"
Leaves whisper softly, gossiping all,
"He's lost to the winds; he'll never stand tall!"

Bark decorated with carvings from a prank,
"Don't carve my name; I'm not in your bank!"
They'd chuckle together at folk who pass by,
As they rustle their needles and let out a sigh.

So here's to the trees, both wise and absurd,
If only we listened, perhaps they'd be heard.
For nature's own humor grows deep in the wood,
In this forest of laughter, they're simply misunderstood!

Nature's Spirals in Stillness

In circles they twist, those trunks on a spree,
Claiming they dance while they stand like a tree.
"I'm grooving to nature's own tranquil beat!"
Said a pine with a grin, tapping roots on the street.

Frustrated branches reach for the sky,
"Don't mind my height, I'm aiming way high!"
But a passing bird mocks, ruffling his feathers,
"You'll never catch clouds, just some shiftless weathers!"

And when autumn comes down with a warm, fiery glow,
The leaves tremble softly, all putting on a show.
"Don't jump! I'm too leafy to dance like a fool,
I'm trying so hard to still look cool!"

A committee of cones debating the scene,
"What's next for our squad? More pine or maraschino?"
Underneath all their chatter, they giggle and chuckle,
For even in stillness, their humor won't buckle!

Constellations Among the Branches

Look up! A pine's telling tales of the night,
With branches as arms stretched out in delight.
"I'm mapping these stars, can you hear my sweet call?"
But a dingy old owl hoots, "Aren't you just tall?"

Pinpricks of light are the dreams of the green,
Who's envious, wishing for glows they've never seen.
"I wish I had sparkles, I want to be bright!"
Said one just a twig with a heart full of fright.

The branches sway gently, crafting sweet lines,
As squirrels debate the best way to climb vines.
They're laughing at stargazers with their heads in the clouds,
While wondering why humans wear tight-fitting shrouds.

So if you're ever caught beneath their wide gaze,
Just chuckle along, finding humor in rays.
For in every pine's story and every soft breeze,
Lies laughter eternal among whispering trees!

Stories Etched in Tree Rings

If bark could talk, what a legend it'd tell,
Of drunken woodpeckers, oh what the swell!
"Once I held a party for critters on high,
A bash full of rumors beneath the blue sky!"

And each ring a memory, impressed with a wink,
"Hoo boy! I chuckled until I couldn't think!
That raccoon stole my sap; I thought we were friends,
But he raided my pantry—where will fun end?"

They argue who's oldest, who's wiser and hence,
Yet newer young sprouts just laugh at their tense.
"Look at those fossils, they think they are shrewd!
They're just wooden relics, missing the good!"

So all rise together with branches held high,
Sharing silly tales, while the breeze hums a sigh.
And as long as they stand, through laughter they cling,
Those stories, evergreen dreams, making the heart sing!

An Album of Rustic Fragrance

In a forest so thick, a woodpecker's beat,
The trees wear their hats, oh, isn't that neat?
Squirrels scamper, they dance with delight,
While pine cones are falling like stars in the night.

The wind sings a tune through the tall, leafy crown,
But wait! Is that pine sap that's dripped on my brown?
It sticks to my shoe, oh what a strange prize,
A sticky reminder of nature's surprise.

Yet laughter erupts at a squirrel's bold feat,
He steals from my sandwich, oh what a cheeky treat!
With a flick and a scurry, he's off like a flash,
While I chase after crumbs, oh what a splash!

Amidst the tall trunks, we share silly tales,
Of deer in pajamas and owls with long wails.
Nature's our stage, where whimsy runs free,
In this album of fragrance, oh come laugh with me!

The Lasting Whisper of Green

Oh pines in a row, with needles so fine,
They whisper in secrets, and sometimes, in rhyme.
A squirrel with swagger, he claims this domain,
Laughing at folks who don't know his name.

The bugs throw a party on branches so high,
While an ant in my sandwich has come by to spy.
A chipmunk's lost snack is a sight to behold,
While pinecone confetti falls down, uncontrolled.

I slip on a needle, take quite the wild ride,
As pines giggle softly, their laughter can't hide.
The trees stand like jesters, in sun's golden sheen,
Here in the kingdom, the laughter's routine.

I join in the fun, with my friends all around,
We're silly and merry, on this soft, earthy ground.
The green grows so loud, it will always be known,
In this lasting embrace, we call it our own.

Pines Against a Fading Sunset

As dusk falls softly, the pines strike a pose,
With shadows that dance, and oh, how it shows!
A raccoon with style, in his evening attire,
Takes center stage, as the twilight grows higher.

The wind plays a tune through the branches all lean,
While I try to catch fireflies, oh, what a scene!
A pinecone rolls past, claiming rights to the floor,
It giggles and teases, then calls out for more.

The sunset glows brighter, a popcorn machine,
While pines poke their heads in the colorful sheen.
With each gentle breeze, the laughter ignites,
As stars peek and wink through the shimm'ring nights.

So let's raise a toast to the pines and their charm,
For they've always kept us both puzzled and warm.
In the fading of light, so much joy can be found,
In the pines' funny antics, we're completely spellbound!

Home to the Lonely Sparrow

In the branches up high, with a chirp and a tweet,
Lives a sparrow so lonely, in search of a treat.
His nest is quite cozy, a small leafy throne,
Yet all he can find are the pine cones alone.

He waits for his friends with a hope in his song,
While squirrels tumble down—oh, life's just so wrong!
Their laughter rings freely, they leap and they dart,
While our poor little sparrow feels left out, oh, the heart!

The wind carries giggles, the pines start to sway,
"Come join us!" they whisper, "Don't let fears weigh!"
But our sparrow just ponders, "Is there room for me?"
In the world of the pines, where is all the glee?

Yet a hush falls around, as night takes its shift,
And with it comes magic, a whimsical gift.
For in cozy old pines, the loneliness fades,
As laughter from nature becomes the parades.

Conversations Among the Canopy

In the breeze, the needles sway,
A chatty flock, hey, let's play!
Squirrels jest and acorns fall,
Who knew trees were so tall?

A whisper here, a giggle there,
Branches stretch, oh, have a care!
"Did you hear the latest joke?"
"Who's the barkiest of the oak?"

Sunlit shards slice through the green,
Every critter's acting keen.
Pinecones tumble, laughter erupts,
Nature's stand-up, all dance and jumps.

So if you wander, heed this call,
Join the fun, come one, come all!
Beneath these trees, oh what a sight,
A canopy that's pure delight!

A Serenade of Starlit Branches

Under stars, the branches sway,
Pine needles twinkle, bright and gay.
"Look at us," the boughs declare,
"Life's a dance, without a care!"

Owls hoot out their serenade,
While crickets chirp, their tunes are played.
"Let's sing all night, we won't tire,
'Cause in this grove, we're on fire!"

The moon peeks through, a curious guest,
Cracks a smile, we're all so blessed.
Pine trees sway with such aplomb,
"Take that, sunset! We'll carry on!"

So next time you stroll through the glade,
Join the trees in their charade.
For in the night, where shadows dance,
Each rustling leaf holds a funny chance!

Between Roots and Skyward Dreams

In the soil, where secrets hide,
Pine roots plot a world so wide.
"Let's grow high, let's touch the sun!"
But what if a bird's the cheeky one?

Branches stretch with lofty schemes,
Grasping at those distant dreams.
"Is that cloud ours or just a tease?"
"Hey, didn't we just catch a breeze?"

The wise old trunk, a gossip king,
Shares tales of love — in ring after ring.
"Did you hear? A squirrel's got style,
He wears a cap, so let's beguile!"

So when you wander, look around,
See the giggles, feel the sound.
In this green world, beneath the beams,
Nature's laughter fuels our dreams!

Invocations of the Forest's Guardians

Oh, mighty pine, we call your name,
With needles sharp, you play the game.
"Protect our woods, keep laughter close,
Tell us stories, we love the most!"

"Who's that creeping?" the pine tree quips,
"Better watch out for those human slips!"
With rustling leaves, they nod along,
In this forest, we all belong.

Owl's the judge, it's wise and grand,
With beady eyes, it takes a stand.
"Respect the trees, our leafy pals,
Let's throw a party, invite the gals!"

So here we gather, with cheers abound,
In the forest where joy is found.
Under the watch of each branching soul,
Together we'll laugh, that's our goal!

The Green Veil of Solitude

In the forest, pines stand tall,
With needles that tickle, seeking a call.
They whisper jokes on a breezy day,
Making squirrels chuckle in their own way.

The sun peeks through, like a shy little sprite,
While pinecones drop down in a comical plight.
These trees play hide and seek with the clouds,
Wearing green hats and laughing out loud.

A porcupine sneezes, the needles a-dance,
The breeze sends a message—the forest's a chance!
To giggle and wiggle under the vast sky,
Where the laughter of nature lets worries pass by.

So come take a stroll through the tall, verdant lanes,
Where humor is rooted and joy gently reigns.
In the shade of the pines, with a grin on your face,
Life's a silly game; it's a charming embrace.

Memories Written in Sap

Beneath the bark, secrets all hide,
In sticky tales where the woodpeckers bide.
Each drip of resin, a story to tell,
Of lovers and squirrels that fell under a spell.

The ants march in lines, a parade on the rise,
While bees buzz along with their clumsy surprise.
An old wind chime swings, with laughter it chimes,
As the trees roll their eyes, not caring for rhymes.

Pine needles cover the ground like a quilt,
With pine-scented dreams that no one has spilt.
They laugh at the daffodils, bright in their cheer,
"Stay away from the forest; the pines like it here!"

So sit by the trunk, feel the sass in the wood,
For even the pines know that laughter is good.
With memories entwined, let your worries all wrap,
In the humor of nature, like jars full of sap.

The Calm Between the Trees

In a hush that giggles, the pines stand in rows,
Tickling the breeze as it swirls and it blows.
"Did you hear," whispered one tree with great pride,
"About the acorn who wanted to glide?"

The ground squirrels chuckled, rolling with glee,
As the pine trees swayed, "Oh, branches, not me!"
A light-hearted spirit danced among leaves,
Beneath the cool boughs, where humor weaves.

The sunlight bursts out, a jester at play,
Flittering shadows that gleefully sway.
the trees crack a smile, they sip on the sun,
In this calm little nook, where laughter's not done.

So step through the woods, let your worries unfurl,
The trees will all salute as you give them a twirl.
Amidst the bold pines, find the fun in the calm,
Join their whimsical dance—nature's joyful balm!

A Dance of Shadows and Light

As dusk falls around, the shadows take flight,
Pines bobbing and weaving in survival's delight.
They throw a big party, all branches in swing,
Inviting the stars for a luminous fling.

The moonbeams giggle as they twirl and they spin,
While fireflies flash, "Let the fun now begin!"
A soft breeze hums a delightfully tune,
In the heart of the forest, where mischief's in bloom.

With pine needles rustling like laughter in play,
Even the crickets jump into ballet.
They leap from one leaf, to another, and cheer,
In a show where the trees bring the joy far and near.

So waltz with the night as shadows take flight,
Join the pine's grand soiree; it feels just right.
In the dance of the woods, let your spirit ignite,
For under the pines, there's pure, silly delight!

www.ingramcontent.com/pod-product-compliance
Lightning Source LLC
Chambersburg PA
CBHW071846160426
43209CB00003B/435